More Mira
of Jesus

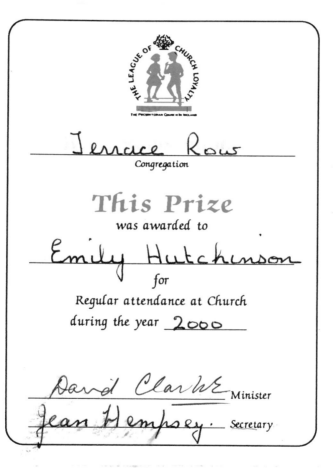

Terrace Row
Congregation

This Prize
was awarded to

Emily Hutchinson
for

Regular attendance at Church
during the year 2000

David Clarke *Minister*

Jean Hempsey. *Secretary*

GOSPEL STANDARD TRUST
PUBLICATIONS
1990

7 Brackendale Grove,
Harpenden, Herts. AL5 3EL.

Jesus' First Miracle

I wonder how many of you have ever been to a wedding? When Jesus was here on earth He was once asked to go to a wedding with His mother and His disciples. So He went. What a good thing it is if we never do anything or go anywhere unless we can ask the Lord Jesus to be with us!

But at this wedding something went wrong. Some mistake had been made. At the meal time there was not enough wine to go round. It must have been very upsetting. Could anything be done?

Mary, the mother of Jesus, knew the answer. She knew that her Son Jesus was also the Son of God. And she knew He would help. So she told those who were there, "Whatever He says to you, do it."

Round the side of the room there were six very large stone pots. This was not surprising for the Jews often kept them in their homes to hold water for washing. But these pots were empty.

Then Jesus asked the people to do a strange thing. "Fill the pots with water," He said. But why water? It was wine they wanted, not water. But they did as Jesus said. They filled the pots with water right up to the brim. If Jesus tells us anything, we should always do it.

Then Jesus told them to draw some out and take it to the man in charge of the meal. He quickly had a taste. What a surprise! It was beautiful. He had never tasted such lovely wine before.

Now the servants had not told the man in charge what had happened. He did not know where they had got the wine. He was very puzzled. He said to the man who was being married, "Can you tell me what has happened? People usually start with the best wine. Then if more is needed it is not so good. But this is delicious. You have kept the best till last."

Yes, Jesus had changed the water into wine. This was the first of His many miracles. His disciples realised that their Master was not just an ordinary man. Who else could turn water into wine?

Jesus can still change things into other things. He is almighty. He can turn sadness into joy. He can change people's lives. He can give us whatever we need. He is "the same yesterday, and today, and for ever."

You can read this story in John, chapter 2, verses 1 to 11.

The Sick Woman

There was once a woman who was very sad. She had been ill for twelve years, and no one could make her better. She had been to all the doctors and spent all her money but no one could help her. She still kept bleeding. She grew worse instead of better.

One day she heard of Jesus. She was told how He could cure sick people. They did not even have to pay. She longed to be made better herself but O! she was so afraid to speak to this wonderful Person.

So she thought of a plan. She would creep up behind Jesus and just touch Him. She had faith to believe that just touching Him would cure her.

But as she went to see Jesus she found there was a crowd of people round about Him. What did she do? Turn round, and go back home? No, she felt she must come to Jesus. God's secret power was drawing her on though she did not know it. She said, "If I can only touch His clothes I shall be better."

At last she came right where Jesus was. She reached out her hand and touched Him, and immediately she knew she was healed. She felt better already. Now she could slip back home without anyone knowing!

But no! The Lord Jesus would not let her do this. She must tell what He had done.

"Who touched Me?" Jesus asked. The disciples

were puzzled. There were crowds around. "Lord, everyone is touching Thee," they said. But this was different. Jesus knows everything, and He knew all that had happened.

At last the poor woman, feeling very frightened, fell down at His feet and told Him everything. Jesus was not angry. He was very, very pleased.

How kindly He spoke to her! "Daughter, be of good comfort. Thy faith hath made thee whole."

It was a happy woman who left the Lord Jesus that day. She had got all that she wanted.

You can read about this miracle in three of the gospels — Matthew, chapter 9, verses 20 to 22; Mark, chapter 5, verses 25 to 34; Luke, chapter 8, verses 43 to 48.

The Poor Boy

There was once a poor boy who was not right in his head. He was a lunatic. Often he had tried to kill himself. Sometimes he would throw himself into water to drown himself, and sometimes he would fall on the fire. Sadly too he could neither hear nor speak. He was deaf and dumb. Think how terrible if you could not speak nor hear any sound.

You can imagine how worried his father was. He had no other children besides this one. Could nothing be done to make him better?

One day the sad father took his son to Jesus' disciples and asked them if they could cure him. But the disciples could not, try as they may. We wonder why the father took the boy to the disciples and not to Jesus Himself? No doubt it was because Jesus had taken Peter, James and John up into the mountain with Him.

As soon as the Lord Jesus came down he saw a crowd of people, arguing and talking. He knew what the matter was. When the people saw the Lord they rushed towards Him. Immediately the father cried, "Master, I brought my son to the disciples but they could not help."

And what a sad tale he told! He told Jesus all about his poor boy growing thinner and thinner, wasting away. Sometimes he foamed at the mouth.

Sometimes he made awful noises with his teeth.

Then Jesus spoke. It was a simple word, but how sweet! "Bring him to Me." We may still bring our troubles to Him.

But even as they were coming the boy fell on the ground in one of his dreadful fits. The sad father knelt at Jesus' feet, longing that He might help. "Lord, if Thou canst do anything, have compassion on us and help us," he cried.

Now he should not have said, "If Thou canst do anything," for the Lord Jesus can do everything. But Jesus was very kind and gracious.

The people all gathered round. What was it that Jesus was saying? He was no longer speaking to the father. "Thou deaf and dumb spirit, come out of him."

Then a strange thing happened. There was a loud noise and the boy fell down on the ground. There he lay completely still. "He is dead!" the people whispered one to another. But he was not dead. He was cured.

Jesus kindly lifted him up and gave him to his father, no longer deaf and dumb or a lunatic. He was better from that moment. We are told the disciples and all the people were "amazed at the mighty power of God" — for Jesus is God.

But what must the father and his son have felt like? What a happy time they must have had as they

went home together! And I am sure they talked about this wonderful Man who had done so much for them.

You can read this story in Matthew, chapter 17, verses 14 to 21; Mark, chapter 9, verses 14 to 29; and Luke, chapter 9, verses 37 to 42.

The Madman

Jesus and His disciples had just sailed across the Sea of Galilee. There had been a dreadful storm but no harm could come to them with Jesus in the ship.

As they climbed out of the ship they saw a strange and frightening sight. What was this creature that was rushing towards them? Surely it was a man? But chains were hanging from his hands and feet and he was not wearing any clothes.

Yes, he was a poor madman. He was plagued by devils who lived inside his heart. What a poor, miserable creature he was! He lived in a gruesome place — in caves where dead bodies were buried. All day and all night long he moaned and cried, cutting himself with stones.

Everybody must have been terrified of him. People had seized him and tied him up, but he soon got free. Even when they tied him up with iron chains he soon broke them.

But now look! As soon as he sees Jesus he runs and falls down at His feet. The power of Jesus could do what those iron chains could never do. The poor man knew that Jesus was the Son of God and even the devils knew so as well.

Then Jesus spoke with power. It was the same voice which spoke when the world was made. Now that voice spoke again. "Come out of the man," He said. And an amazing thing happened. All the devils fled and went into a herd of pigs that was feeding up on the mountain.

The mountain side was very steep and went right down to the sea. With a great rush all the pigs hurtled down the slope into the water and were drowned. There were about two thousand of them altogether.

The pig keepers were so frightened that they ran away. But not the poor man. How happy he was! He just sat there, quiet and peaceful, looking at Jesus and listening to Him.

Soon lots of people came hurrying along. They had heard about the strange things that had happened. But now they could hardly believe their eyes. There he was, that terrible man who was never still! That man who had frightened everybody! But there he was sitting quietly at Jesus' feet. And he was wearing clothes. (Where he got them from we do not know.)

It must have been the happiest day in the poor madman's life. But there was just something which made him a little sad. This wonderful Saviour, the Lord Jesus, was now going back across to the other side of the lake.

If only he could go with Him! He begged that he might. But no! Jesus had something for him to do. "Go home to your friends, and tell them the great things the Lord has done for you."

Yes, Jesus did great things when here on earth. Healing the madman was a great thing. Dying on the cross to save His people was an even greater thing. He still does great things today.

How wonderful if we can say, "The Lord has done great things for us, whereof we are glad!"

You can read this story in Mark, chapter 5, verses 1 to 20, and in Luke, chapter 8, verses 26 to 39.

Walking on the Sea

It was the end of the day and Jesus and His disciples stood by the side of the Sea of Galilee.

"Get into the ship, and sail across to the other side," Jesus told them. As they climbed in and got ready to sail, they noticed that He was not coming with them. As they watched He walked all alone to the top of the mountain. I wonder why He was going there? It was because He wanted to be by Himself, to talk to His Father in heaven.

When night fell the disciples were in the middle of the sea. It began to get very windy. Soon a storm broke. The wind grew louder and rough waves began to shake the ship.

The disciples were frightened. They rowed as hard as they could but made no headway. The wind was too strong for them. Worst of all Jesus was not with them. If He had been with them they knew that all must be well.

But do you know? Jesus was watching them. They could not see Him but up in the mountain He could see them. His loving eyes were upon them. He always sees His people in their troubles. It does not matter where they are or how far away.

Still the disciples struggled on. I think they were hoping that Jesus would come to them — but how could He? There was no way. But how wonderful!

Nothing can ever stop Jesus coming to help. And He is never too late.

Then the Lord Jesus did something no one had ever done before. He walked on the sea. You know that no one can walk on water. It is impossible. If you try to walk on water you sink. But what no one else could do Jesus did.

Suddenly the disciples saw an amazing sight. It was now very dark and they had waited such a long time. But someone was coming towards them across the stormy waves. Who could it be? They were terrified. They thought it was a ghost.

But then this figure called to them, so kindly: "Be of good cheer: it is I; be not afraid." And they knew straight away who it was.

When we are afraid we need to ask Jesus to come and help us. Do you know the little hymn about Jesus walking on the sea? One verse says,

"Thus, when the storm of life is high,
Come, Saviour, to my aid;
Come, when no other help is nigh,
And say, 'Be not afraid.'"

But now He did not leave them. He went with them into the ship, and as soon as He entered the ship the wind stopped blowing and the sea became calm. In no time they were at the other side of the sea. They had arrived safely.

What lessons they had learned! Jesus had not failed them. He had not forgotten about them. But above all they knew who their Lord and Master was. They said to Him, "Of a truth Thou art the Son of God."

You can read this story in Matthew, chapter 14, verses 22 to 33; Mark, chapter 6, verses 45 to 52; and John, chapter 6, verses 15 to 21.

The Centurion's Servant

There were all kinds of people who came to Jesus to help them — and He did not refuse any. One of them was a Roman soldier. He was an important man because he had a hundred soldiers under him. He was called a centurion.

This centurion had such wonderful faith that Jesus was amazed. How did a soldier, belonging to the enemies of God's people, come to have such faith? God gave it to him.

So we find he was a very kind man. Many soldiers are cruel, but not this centurion. He loved God's people. He even built them a place where they could worship God, and paid for it himself.

But now he was in trouble. One of his slaves was ill. Most Romans did not bother about their slaves, or even got rid of them if they were unwell. But not this centurion. Why, he spoke about the poor slave as if he were his own son.

Now, though the centurion was a great man, he did not think he was good enough to go to Jesus. Jesus was great and holy, the Son of God, and the centurion felt that he himself was weak and sinful.

So he asked other people to go to Jesus for help. He told them to tell Jesus that he was just not good enough to go to Him. The people could not help telling Jesus all the good things he had done — but

that was not how the centurion felt.

How wonderful the message he sent to Jesus! He said, "If I tell someone to come, he comes. He dare not disobey. Or if I tell someone else to go, immediately he goes." He knew that all Jesus needed to do was just to speak, and the slave would be better.

All things do obey the Lord Jesus. To make the world, "He spoke, and it was done." So the soldier knew that if Jesus just spoke, illness must obey Him and go away. "Speak the word only, Lord, and my servant shall be healed."

What a miracle this was! Jesus made the poor servant better (and he was dying!) without even going to see him. So what a happy end to the story! We read: "Returning to the house they found the servant whole that had been sick."

Jesus now lives in heaven. Do you ever pray to Him? When you do, remember His wonderful power. When He speaks, all things have to obey.

You can read this story in Matthew, chapter 8, verses 5 to 13, and in Luke, chapter 7, verses 1 to 10.

The Old Lady

You have all heard about Peter and the things he did. He was one of Jesus' disciples. He was the one who said to Jesus, "Thou art the Christ, the Son of the living God." Once he found a piece of money in a fish's mouth. Once he cut off a man's ear.

But did you know that Peter was married? that he had a wife? and that they had a home in Capernaum? and that an old lady lived with them, Peter's wife's mother? Did you know that?

Most of the stories about Jesus and Peter happened on the lake or by the lake side, but this one took place inside Peter's house. We do not know anything about Peter's wife, but we are told about her mother.

One day Jesus came to this house. He loved to be with Peter, and Peter loved to be with Him. But today someone was missing. Where was the old lady, Peter's wife's mother?

Quickly Jesus was told that she was ill. She was in bed. She felt burning hot — as people often do when they are not well. She was suffering from a fever.

Jesus loved to perform His miracles of love. So today He came where the old lady was lying sick. Very kindly and gently He touched her hand. And immediately she felt better.

When most people have had a fever it takes a day or two to get over it. But not in this case! Jesus'

cures are perfect.   A minute or two later she was up and about the house, helping with the work.

Do you know the little hymn:

> "Jesus is a wise Physician,
>   Skilful and exceeding kind"?

He can heal both body and soul.   And His cures are always perfect.

You can read this story in Matthew, chapter 8, verses 14 and 15; Mark, chapter 1, verses 29 to 31; and Luke, chapter 4, verses 38 and 39.

The Widow's Son

One day Jesus and His disciples went to visit a city called Nain. A crowd of people went with them. Perhaps they were hoping to see another of Jesus' wonderful miracles.

But what is this procession coming towards them out of the city gate? The people are walking slowly. They look sad. And what is it they are carrying?

Yes, it was a sad procession, and one woman in the procession was specially sad. She had no husband; she was a widow. And now she had lost her son.

We do not know how old he was, or what was his name, but he was her only son, and he had died. Now they were carrying him out to bury him for the graves were usually outside the city wall. No wonder his mother was so sad.

How sorry Jesus felt for her! And what a kind word He spoke to her: "Weep not! Do not cry!" But how could she help crying?

Then Jesus put His hand on the coffin. Everyone was amazed. What was He going to do? They all stood perfectly still.

Then He spoke to the young man who was dead. "Arise!" He said. And the dead man obeyed. Is it possible he is really alive? Yes, he is sitting up. Now he is beginning to talk. And Jesus gave him back to his mother. I am sure she never had such a

lovely present before.

Soon all through the country people were talking about the Lord's kindness and His power.

He loves to make sad people happy, especially those who are sad because they have sinned against Him. He says, "Come unto Me, all ye that labour and are heavy laden, and I will give you rest."

You can read this story in Luke, chapter 7, verses 11 to 16.

The Crooked Woman

There was once a crooked woman. Her poor back was out of shape so that she was bent double. Her head was down towards the ground and she could not look up. It must have been a very sad sight. And she had been like it for many years.

Have you noticed that the people Jesus made better were people that no one else could help?

Well, it was the Sabbath day and when Jesus saw this poor woman His heart was filled with pity. He called to her to come to Him. It must have been with very feeble steps she came. But as she came Jesus said, "Woman, thou art loosed from thine infirmity." Then He placed His kind hands on her and immediately she was better. She could stand up straight. She was no longer bowed down. She could walk properly.

And what do you think was the first thing that she did? Yes, she thanked and praised God for what He had done. Don't we need to be thankful if we are well when so many people suffer?

Yet Jesus had many enemies. Some of them grumbled because Jesus had made the crooked woman better on the Sabbath day. It is hard to understand them, isn't it? We believe we must keep the Sabbath day as God has said: "Remember the Sabbath day to keep it holy." But is it not keeping it

holy when Jesus does wonderful things? Why, said Jesus, you set free your donkey or your cow on the Sabbath and take it to have something to drink! And why should I not set free this woman who has been ill so long?

Some girls and boys know our lives are crooked through sin. But they know that Jesus the Saviour can make the crooked straight. "He is able to save unto the uttermost."

You can read this story in Luke, chapter 13, verses 10 to 17.

The Raising of Lazarus

Perhaps the most wonderful of all Jesus' miracles was the bringing of His friend Lazarus back to life.

Close to Jerusalem was a little town called Bethany. Here two sisters lived together with their brother. Their names were Martha, Mary and Lazarus. And Jesus dearly loved them. Bethany was a very special place to Him. So many people treated Him badly but here at Bethany Jesus was always a welcome visitor.

One day Lazarus was very ill. His sisters were sad. They could see he was not getting better. So they sent a message to Jesus: "Lord, he whom Thou lovest is sick."

How strange! When Jesus heard the news He stopped where He was for another two days. You would have thought He would have hurried to Bethany at once, wouldn't you? But He didn't. Often we cannot understand things the Lord does but He never makes a mistake.

By this time Lazarus was dead. Jesus knew this for He knows everything. At last He told His disciples, "Lazarus is dead," but He said, "Let us go to him." Why go to see Lazarus now he was dead?

When Jesus arrived at Bethany the body of Lazarus had been in the grave for four days. But Martha was so pleased to hear that Jesus had come.

She ran to meet Him. "Lord," she cried, "if Thou hadst been here my brother would not have died." And when Mary saw Him she said just the same.

We are told that "Jesus wept." His kind heart was filled with both love and sadness for His friends. As well as being God He was a real Man. But was it not too late now? Was it possible that Jesus could bring him back to life?

Everyone went to the grave. It was a cave and a big stone was in front. "Take it away," said Jesus. Then with a loud voice He called, "Lazarus, come forth!" and an amazing thing happened. The dead man came out wrapped up in grave clothes. It must have been hard for him to walk for they were like bandages tied round him. Jesus said, "Take them off him so that he can be free."

No, Jesus was not too late. He has power even over death. Soon He Himself was to die on the cross, but no man or woman could come to His grave and cry, "Come forth." He did not need it. He rose by His own power. He still lives today.

You can read this story in John, chapter 11, verses 1 to 46.